W0005891

A Center for Soulful Living Publication

For information address the Center for Soulful Living, P. O. Box 583, St. George, UT 84771-0583, USA, www.aboutcsl.com.

ISBN 0-9765138-4-6   Made in USA

5. At the end of each alone time, find one thought to take away with you. Perhaps it will be a thought like "I'm more deserving than I thought." Keep it as your "thought for the day," a slogan or motto to recall.

4. *Develop a dialogue with your self, just like you'd talk with a friend. Tell yourself what you think, want or need … then listen attentively. Soon you'll notice that you actually do have a new friend—your self.*

3. Once you've made the connection, ask your self questions—such as who am I, what am I like, why am I worth believing in. Then, listen again, acutely—you may be surprised at the answers. You'll start to appreciate yourself like you never have before.

2. *During this alone time make an intimate connection with your special self. Listen sensitively to your body, emotions, heart and soul as they speak. If at first you don't feel the connection, keep listening ... more deeply.*

1. Spend quiet, alone time with yourself every day—just with your self. For five or fifteen minutes, use your pen ... stay with your thoughts ... rely on your feelings ... listen to your intuition—whatever style is best for being alone with the world's most important person—you!

The "How to" of Valuing Yourself
Five Steps

8. I choose to live a life of miracles and extra-ordinary experiences. I expect that my life will work, and will work exceptionally well. I intend a life filled with everything I need to make me happy. I won't settle for less ... I'm shooting for the stars.

7. From now on I will look at my life from above the forest. I will see the bigger picture, the greater meanings and purposes. I will choose innovative thinking and creative interpretations.

6. *I look first and foremost to myself for the solutions to my needs. I refuse to give my power away to or feel less than anyone else. I am enough in and of myself, with all the resources I need. I trust myself and my own wisdom to see me through anything.*

5. *For every situation I will look for solutions, answers, options. I refuse to sit back, be passive, feel bewildered, or go numb. I will get busy, be involved, and dedicate myself—right away.*

4. I see every circumstance and event as an opportunity, a gift, a blessing, an invitation to something new and extraordinary.

3. *I claim my birthright—the right to be powerful and in charge. I deserve it, and it's mine. From now on, I will succeed. I refuse to hold back, no matter how afraid I may be. I'm powerful every minute of every day, period—case closed.*

2. I choose to live free of all negative thoughts or feelings. Whenever they enter my mind, I will immediately say "no!" and command them away.

1. I choose to eliminate all negative thoughts from my mind. I will not feel sorry for myself … criticize or blame others … complain … or see myself as a helpless victim, no matter what.

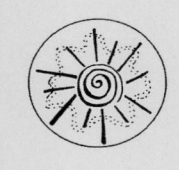

*Dorothy's Eight Attitudes
from Over the Forest*

10. Once you get the hang of a new attitude, practice it even more. With more focus and practice, you can get really good at it. Remember, you can become a totally positive, healthy thinker.

9. *If you fail or fall flat on your face, pick yourself up right away. Please don't feel sorry for yourself, complain or feel like a victim. Instead of those old attitudes, start over, become your own champion.*

8. *Thank your mind for its hard work, for the ways it's helping you. Your expression of gratitude may be the start of a new friendship, a more cooperative relationship between you and your mind.*

7. Pick a difficult situation—one where you feel powerless or afraid. Develop a new attitude: Decide what attitudes you need to help you in this situation … and instruct your mind accordingly.

6. *Write a list of attitudes that you want in your life—ones you really need. Read this list every day … practice them every day. Revise them as necessary. Remind yourself of them regularly.*

5. *Be determined that it will work. Never give up or stop. Develop this super-attitude:*
I am the master of my mind's every thought.
I'm in charge of my attitudes.
I have Oz power in my thinking.

4. Talk to your mind. Tell it how you want it to think, to interpret the circumstances of your life, to help you. Be specific, direct and strong with your mind.

3. Imagine yourself as an employer, supervisor or commanding officer instructing your recruit, employee or trainee about how to think. Get the idea? You have the authority. You're in charge.

2. Realize that your attitude is 100 percent controllable. You can master every one of your thoughts. Though it may look difficult, you can control your thinking successfully.

1. *Ask yourself: "Do I really want to be in charge of my mind and thoughts? Take charge not because you think you should, but because you want to. Reach inside and discover how strongly you want a healthy attitude.*

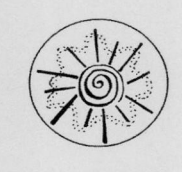

Taking Charge of Your Attitude
A Ten Point Approach

3. Finally, once your "yes!" is in place, watch what happens. Notice how whatever help you need just starts to show up ... how you find the exact experiences that will lead you to your goal.

2. Then, say a giant "yes!" to that invitation. A really powerful "yes!" A resounding "yes!"—one that means, "I refuse to hold back. I'm going for it. I'm jumping in all the way." Be committed to succeeding.

Once you hear that signal, pay attention—your heart is offering you an invitation, and it's nice to know what you're being invited to.

1. Listen closely to life's invitations. Sometimes, they hit you strongly over the head. More often, however, you'll hear them rumbling down there in your heart before they register clearly in your mind.

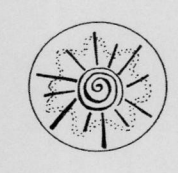

Three Steps to a Life of Power

10. *Are you expecting a miracle ... looking for extraordinary results in your life ... "going for" complete and total happiness?*

9. Do you trust yourself and your own instincts to see you through? Do you have confidence in life to support and help you?

8. *Are you going for it every day … not holding back … making it happen … putting your strategies into action … really doing it?*

7. Are you clear about how to take charge? Do you understand how to make your life powerful? Do you know your strategy for winning?

6. Do you intend to be totally in charge of every aspect of your life? Are you affirming that what you want to happen will happen?

5. *Are you ready to stop looking outside of yourself for the answers to your needs ... ready to rely on your own wisdom to see you through?*

4. Are you committed to owning your Oz power ... determined to take charge ... saying "yes!" to being powerful every day?

3. Do you really want to be that powerful …
to be the master of every day of your life?
Can you feel that "want" stirring inside you?

2. *Do you believe that you deserve to claim that power ... that you have the right to use it to make yourself happy?*

1. Do you believe that you're innately powerful
... that power lives and breathes inside you ...
that you have magical slippers on your feet?

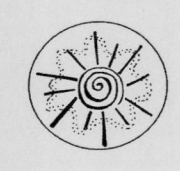

The Oz Power Quiz
Ten questions about your Oz Power

HUMANHOOD

LIVING WITH
OZ POWER

SAGEHOOD: ABOVE THE FOREST OF OZ

Enjoy! Enjoy! Enjoy!

*Just like Dorothy, you're always supported …
you always land on your feet.*

*So, kick back … relax … and enjoy your ride
through life.*

Try just "being" for awhile, instead of doing or thinking. See what happens.

Your own wisdom will fill that empty space with its special secrets.

Pull back from life's conflicts and dramas.
Instead, just relax with them.

Once you do, you've arrived over the forest.

Notice the beauty that lives around you —in nature, persons and events.

Learn beauty's special language—feel it, experience it, touch it, treasure it.

Try not judging others. Look beyond appearances, and find their truth.

Find peace with their external "stuff" —you know, it's not important anyway.

A sage is a person of vision and wisdom. These qualities live in you too.

Say "yes!" to your bigger vision and to your heart centered wisdom.

Quit trying to control your life's circumstances. Instead, try enjoying them.

Accept life—in whatever way lets you enjoy its daily pleasures.

Be simply who you are. Not who you—or others—think you should be.

Just be yourself. That's when you can hear your own wisdom.

Let go of your value judgments, your pet theories, your prized biases.

Once you are free of them, you'll discover a bigger vision—inside yourself.

Stop complaining about your struggles. Be thankful for all your difficulties.

They're what made you who you are. They help you to find your true "self."

Don't take it all so seriously. Remember, life is mainly a creative journey.

Experience your life in a lighter, freer way. Try even being amused by it.

You have the right to be fully happy. Your own wisdom can lead you there.

Every day, say to yourself: "I choose to be peaceful … to live in my heart!"

SAGEHOOD

ABOVE THE FOREST OF OZ

Life is ultimately about making miracles commonplace. Ask for miracles.

Keep clicking your heels, with trust, until your miracles become real.

Click your heels … as often as you want … to create what you want.

Why? Because you can, because you want to, because it's your right.

Picture yourself already being an "in charge" adult, even if not fully.

That picture alone can carry you a long way. Let go of out-of-date pictures.

Don't forget—adulthood means enjoying the freedom you fought hard for.

It's not all responsibility—it's also fun! So enjoy it! Have fun! You deserve it.

Take responsibility for everything in your life. No exceptions ... no excuses!

"The buck stops here"—you're willing to take charge of everything you do.

Intend that what you want will happen. Expect it; affirm it; and will it.

When you affirm what you want, you're setting the stage for it to occur.

Make bold decisions about what to do and how to behave. You're the boss.

If something you're doing doesn't feel right or helpful, change it—right away.

Take charge of your mind; guide your thoughts; and choose your beliefs.

You're in charge of your mind.

"Want" authority over your life. "Will" yourself to be master of your destiny.

Embrace your deep desire for personal power. Feel the power of wanting.

Believe in yourself. Believe in your right to have power over your whole life.

Believe that you are entitled to your dreams. Believe ... believe ... believe.

You create your own destiny. That's the truth. Believe it; accept it; and own it.

Once you believe that your destiny is up to you, you'll start to feel in charge.

Always keep your sights on your power. Never forget, you're in charge.

Go for being fully and totally empowered every day. It will work.

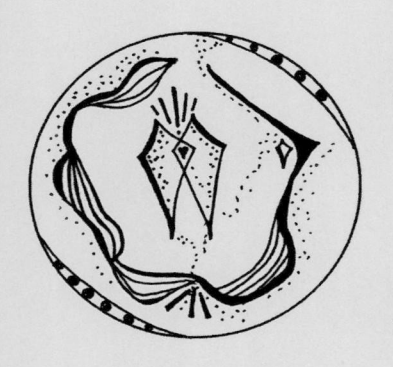

ADULTHOOD

OWNING PERSONAL POWER

You deserve victory and freedom. Never stop believing in your deservingness.

Even if you fall on your face, start over … knowing that you're worth it.

Being open and trusting never means being passive and permissive.

If it feels like a sign of weakness, maybe you're being too selfless.

When we let go, a greater wisdom takes over and creates our next steps.

You can feel less responsible for those steps. Enjoy letting go!

No matter how scary the Wicked Witch is, remind yourself of this truth:

Life wants you to win, and life will help you win. Turn to life—use it.

See life as a cherished friend, helper and support.

Just as you would with a friend, talk to life, appreciate life, invite life.

Flowing with life means that you're living with a power bigger than yourself.

Accept that power in your life. Find it in the simple happenings of each day.

Trust life also. Notice how life supports you and takes care of you every day.

Once you notice this support, invite yourself to believe it and to look for it.

The key to trusting yourself is first to love yourself unconditionally.

Stop judging or finding fault with yourself. Love yourself as you are.

Trust yourself—even if you've learned not to do so.

You'll probably find that you can trust yourself a lot.

Believe in your own instincts, your intuitive hunches, your natural reactions.

Chances are they're usually more accurate than you think they are.

Stay open to success. Believe in yourself and your right to succeed.

Your freedom is worth pursuing. Don't doubt yourself.

Letting go means giving up trying to control those around you.

Let others be the way they are. Stop trying to change them.

Reach out to your friends or family for emotional support and sound advice.

Ask one person to support you lovingly and another to guide you objectively.

In defeating your Wicked Witch, become even more responsible for your life.

Freedom without responsibility often creates another unwanted Witch.

If you're angry, accept your anger as a helpful tool in your quest for freedom.

And invite it to be short-lived. A little anger is good; too much makes you sick.

What's your plan? Your strategy? Is it clear and defined enough?

If you know what you're doing, your chances of success are increased.

Do you really want to be totally free? Or are you rebelling out of frustration?

If you're mainly looking for revenge, chances are you'll not get free.

How committed to success are you? 50 percent? 100 percent? Be honest.

Don't leap forward until your resolve is strong enough to see you through.

Even if your Wicked Witch is external, you're still part of the solution.

You always have to change yourself as well as the external situation.

Be clear about what you're breaking free of. Know who the Wicked Witch is.

Ask yourself: is the real cause of my pain outside of me, or is it an inside job?

Always remember your goal—you're working for your freedom, nothing less.

Don't let any distraction get in your way or move you off track.

No matter how scary it is, remember—you can overcome the Wicked Witch!

You can do it. You really can! Don't give up. Keep moving forward.

You have a right—and a duty—to grow up. Nobody stays the same forever.

Being a child is fun for a while, but staying there too long becomes boring.

ADOLESCENCE

BREAKING FREE

Believe in yourself. Believe in your worth. Believe in your right to be happy.

Believe in your potential. Believe in your splendor. Above all else, believe!

Ask yourself: how much do I really want my dreams to come true?

When you're clear about the answer, go for it. Don't get discouraged.

Never blame others for your misfortunes. Instead, look for solutions.

You can fix the problem and right the wrong —simply by taking charge.

Take responsibility for everything you do.
Admit being wrong if you are.

You're responsible for how your life turns out—
every minute of every day.

Stop feeling like a victim. Stop thinking like a victim. Stop being a victim.

You never have been and never will be a victim—unless you think you are.

What are you saying "yes!" to? To power or poverty? To health or sickness?

To strength or weakness? If you don't like your answer, change your vote.

Adopt this attitude: you, and only you, make the decisions that guide your life.

You're responsible for every choice in your life. Be clear, focused and strong.

Take charge of your body—your health, eating, symptoms, exercise.

It's your body; you're responsible for it. Be a good friend; make it healthy.

Take charge of your emotions. Become the master of your inner hurts.

Command any pain filled feelings inside you to find healing and strength.

Take charge of your mind—your thoughts, attitudes and judgments.

Train your mind to think exactly the way you want it to.

Some situations can be intimidating. Don't hold back. Meet them head on.

Be daring. Act courageously and assertively, no matter how scared you are.

Whenever you feel personal power lacking, call it to you ... until you feel it.

Your personal power is there to help you. "Don't leave home without it."

Remind yourself that today you're the master of your destiny.

You're the CEO of the company called "you." You're in charge.

Just as you have a right to love, it's also your birthright to be powerful.

It's what you were created for—to own your power. Claim your birthright.

Listen to your "gut"—it's there that you can feel the stirrings of your power.

This is your core and foundation. Stand solidly in it—feel its grounded roar.

Love lives in your body as well as in your heart. Learn to love your body.

Listen to its loving messages, its subtle signals, its caring embrace.

Feel your emotions. Your feelings are a valuable, important part of you.

Experience and honor them—they're an intimate part of your happiness.

Experience others' feelings—their joy and pain, their needs and doubts.

When you walk in their shoes and share their life, magical effects occur.

See everybody's faults through the eyes of love.

Try understanding instead of seeing "what's wrong."

Treasure your friends and loved ones. Don't take them for granted.

It's so healing to be loved. Take really good care of your close relationships.

Love is alive and well all around you—in nature, food, pets and people.

It wants to nourish your heart and soul. Feel its nurturing touch and caress.

Forgive everyone in your life. Harboring resentments hurts only yourself.

Forgive them all—parents, siblings, enemies— with everything you've got.

Forgive yourself—for everything … that's right, everything.

No matter what you've done, you deserve a new life. So let the past go.

Care about yourself, first and foremost. Treat yourself as deserving.

Others usually value you only to the degree that you value yourself.

Bring love into your mind. Make it an intimate part of your thinking.

Let your sensitivity and compassion influence all your thoughts and beliefs.

Invite love to heal your emotional pain. Pour love into your inner wounds.

Keep loving them until they "feel" your love more strongly than their pain.

Love is all about seeing the beauty around you. You're beautiful. So is life.

With love as your guide, see beauty every-where, in everything, all the time.

Look at everyone through the eyes of love. Give them the benefit of the doubt.

You can see their lovable, positive qualities—if you're open to seeing them.

Listen closely to your heart—it speaks to you about how to love.

Your heart has its own way of talking to you. Learn its soft, special language.

"Hang in there" until you find your answer, solution or truth. Don't give up!

Stopping in mid-stream just means you'll have to start over again later.

*Look at every issue from "over the forest"
—there you'll find the bigger picture.*

There's no substitute for a large vision.

Ignorance is not bliss. If you don't have enough information, acquire it.

Develop your understanding of everything that's important to you.

Following your natural intuitions and hunches usually works best.

Trust your own personal "sense"—it can lead you to the best answer.

Make your assumptions and attitudes as big and broad as possible.

These subtle influences, if narrow or bigoted, can keep you from enjoying life.

Stretch your mind. Look for alternatives or more creative ways of thinking.

If you do, you'll keep your thinking fresh, up-to-date, and more exciting.

Say "yes!" to your dreams. Say "yes!" to your deservingness.

Say "yes!" to living as you want. Say "yes!" to life.

Be a believer. Believe in and value life, people, and whatever matters to you.

Above, all, believe in who you are, not who you think you "should" be.

Ask yourself: "What do I need right now?" Then ask it again … and again.

Sometimes, the answers you need show up only when you stay focused.

Always be clear about what you want—for your life, for this year, for today.

Your desires and dreams usually come true when you're clear.

Confusion isn't helpful at all.

If you're confused, identify what's confusing, and get clear.

You have a personal style for finding your own answers, solutions and truths.

Discover that style and own it—it's your personal road map to happiness.

Your mind is a powerful tool.

Learn how it works, and you can build a powerful life.

Use the resources around you—friends' advice, helpful books, useful theories.

But use them to enhance your inner knowing. Above all, listen to yourself.

Think positively. Negative thinking only wears you out and discourages you.

Stay focused on the positive side of life—it's your key to creating real solutions.

SCHOOLING

LEARNING THE PLANET'S THREE C'S

Choose only situations where you will be respected, cared for, and valued.

You deserve it—so, change jobs, friends or circumstances, if necessary.

Guilt is mostly unhelpful to you.

Comply because you want to or choose to—not out of guilt or obligation.

Fear can weaken you. Obey those in authority, but don't obey your fears.

Face every fear head on. Conform on the outside; take charge on the inside.

Serving others can have great benefits—love, approval and security.

Drink in these "pluses." You earned them.

Being the power behind the throne can be just as powerful as sitting on the throne.

Support whoever is on the throne—and feel proud of yourself for doing it.

Compliance can be a sign not of weakness, but of true empowerment.

Believe this with all your heart—you're as powerful as the one you're serving.

Stop complaining, criticizing or rebelling. It will only make you feel worse.

Take charge of your situation by being the best that you can be.

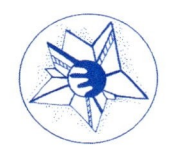

You are not a victim, except in your mind. You never have been or will be.

With all your will, refuse to feel like a victim. Find your strength, deep inside.

Conformity can be your own choice as much as a role imposed on you.

When you're choosing to conform, you become the boss … you're in charge!

How you feel about yourself is as important as how safe or secure you are.

Value yourself ... see your worth ... know your greatness—no matter what!

You're unique and special no matter what your position in life. Love yourself.

Never lose yourself ... above all, please respect yourself.

CHILDHOOD

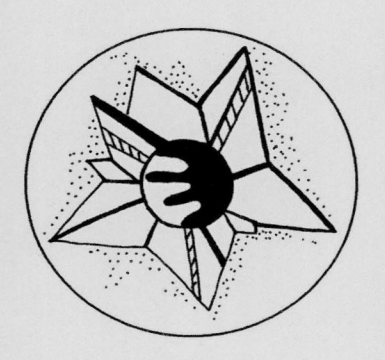

SURVIVING IN A STRANGE WORLD

You really can make your life work. Believe in yourself, with all your heart.

Keep reminding yourself—you're the hero of your life. You can do this.

Don't forget—you have your own ruby red slippers; they're on your feet.

Even if you haven't discovered their special powers, keep looking for them!

Remember—Dorothy learned all about Oz by walking its scary path.

You can learn a lot about yourself—by walking headlong into your life.

Get clear about what you're afraid of. Make your fears more tangible.

Vague anxieties are more difficult to conquer than clear-cut issues.

*Don't let fear drive your life or be a nagging
back seat driver!*

*Put yourself behind the wheel and drive …
drive to your heart's content.*

Whatever you're afraid of, don't run from it. Look it squarely in the eye.

You'll get farther if you face it head on than if you avoid it.

Life here isn't necessarily as serious or stressful as you think.

Lighten up—picture your life as lighter, more flowing—and see how it feels.

Your fear is a good sign. It means that you're a feeling, caring person.

Be proud of your sensitive feelings—they will soon become your strength.

The truth about you is this: You were born to take charge of your fears.

It's your birthright to trust in yourself and to be in charge of your life.

You have more power to draw on than you think. You were born with it.

It's "in reserve" inside you. Keep looking for it —you'll find it.

Remember—everyone else around you is just as afraid of life as you are.

They're just better at hiding it. You're not alone.

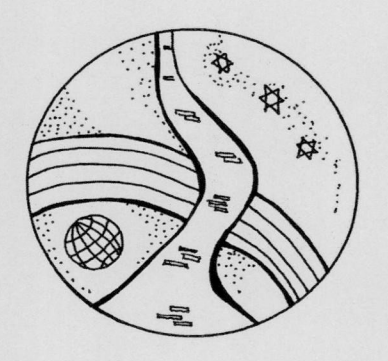

BIRTH

ARRIVING IN THE LAND OF OZ

CONTENTS